Zoo Animals

Sea Lion

Patricia Whitehouse

Heinemann Library
Chicago, Illinois

D1411121

© 2003 Reed Educational & Professional Publishing
Published by Heinemann Library,
an imprint of Reed Educational & Professional Publishing,
Chicago, Illinois

Customer Service 888-454-2279
Visit our website at www.heinemannlibrary.com

All rights reserved. No part of this publication may be reproduced or transmitted in any form or by any means, electronic or mechanical, including photocopying, recording, taping, or any information storage and retrieval system, without permission in writing from the publisher.

Designed by Sue Emerson, Heinemann Library
Printed and bound in China by South China Printing Company

07 06
10 9 8 7 6 5 4

Library of Congress Cataloging-in-Publication Data
Whitehouse, Patricia, 1958-
     Sea lion / Patricia Whitehouse.
        p. cm. — (Zoo animals)
Includes index.
Summary: An introduction to sea lions, including their size, diet and everyday life style, which highlights differences between those in the wild and those living in zoo habitat.
    ISBN: 1-58810-902-X (HC), 1-40340-647-2 (Pbk.)
    1. Sea lions—Juvenile literature. [1. Sea lions. 2. Zoo animals.] I. Title.
    QL737.P63 W52 2002
    599.79'75—dc21

                          2001007438

Acknowledgments
The author and publishers are grateful to the following for permission to reproduce copyright material:
Title page, pp. 6, 22, 24 Ken Lucas/Visuals Unlimited; p. 4 Barbara Gerlach/DRK Photo; p. 5 James Lemass/Index Stock Imagery; p. 7 David J. Wrobel/Visuals Unlimited; p. 8 Wayne Lynch/DRK Photo; p. 9 Joe McDonald/Corbis; p. 10 Tom & Pat Leeson/DRK Photo; p. 11L Buddy Mays/Corbis; p. 11R Konrad Wothe/Minden Pictures; p. 12 Doug Perrine/DRK Photo; p. 13 James Marshall/Corbis; pp. 14, 20 Chicago Zoological Society/The Brookfield Zoo; p. 15 Gail Mooney/Corbis; p. 16 John Gerlach/DRK Photo; pp. 17, 18 Ken Lucas/Visuals Unlimited; p. 19 Will Troyer/Visuals Unlimited; p. 21 Richard T. Nowitz/Photo Reseachers, Inc.; p. 23 (row 1, L-R) Tom & Pat Leeson/DRK Photo, Corbis, David J. Wrobel/Visuals Unlimited; p. 23 (row 2, L-R) David J. Wrobel/Visuals Unlimited, Wayne Lynch/DRK Photo, William Jorgensen/Visuals Unlimited; p. 23 (row 3, L-R) Ken Lucas/Visuals Unlimited, Greg Probst/Corbis, Jim Schulz/Chicago Zoological Society/The Brookfield Zoo; back cover (L-R) Joe McDonald/Corbis, David J. Wrobel/Visuals Unlimited

Cover photograph by Chicago Zoological Society/The Brookfield Zoo
Photo research by Bill Broyles

Every effort has been made to contact copyright holders of any material reproduced in this book.
Any omissions will be rectified in subsequent printings if notice is given to the publisher.

Special thanks to our advisory panel for their help in the preparation of this book:
Eileen Day, Preschool Teacher
Chicago, IL

Ellen Dolmetsch,
Library Media Specialist
Wilmington, DE

Kathleen Gilbert,
Teacher
Round Rock, TX

Sandra Gilbert,
Library Media Specialist
Houston, TX

Angela Leeper,
Educational Consultant
North Carolina Department
of Public Instruction
Raleigh, NC

Pam McDonald, Reading Teacher
Winter Springs, FL

Melinda Murphy,
Library Media Specialist
Houston, TX

We would also like to thank Lee Haines, Assistant Director of Marketing and Public Relations at the Brookfield Zoo in Brookfield, Illinois, for his review of this book.

Some words are shown in bold, like this.
You can find them in the picture glossary on page 23.

Contents

What Are Sea Lions?

Sea lions are **mammals.**

Mammals have hair or fur on their bodies.

In the wild, sea lions live near the ocean.

But you can see sea lions at the zoo.

What Do Sea Lions Look Like?

flipper

Sea lions have brown hair on their bodies.

They have four **flippers**.

snout | whiskers | ear flap

Sea lions have whiskers on their **snouts.**

They have **ear flaps** on their heads.

What Do Baby Sea Lions Look Like?

A baby sea lion looks like its parents, but it is smaller.

Baby sea lions are called **pups**.

New pups are light brown.

They look more like their parents as they get older.

Where Do Sea Lions Live?

In the wild, sea lions live in the ocean and on the **shore**.

They live in groups called **colonies**.

In the zoo, sea lions live in
big pools.

Many of these pools have
underwater windows.

What Do Sea Lions Eat?

In the wild, sea lions find fish
and **squid** to eat.

At the zoo, **zookeepers** feed sea lions fish and squid.

What Do Sea Lions Do All Day?

Sea lions eat during the day.

They also swim and sleep.

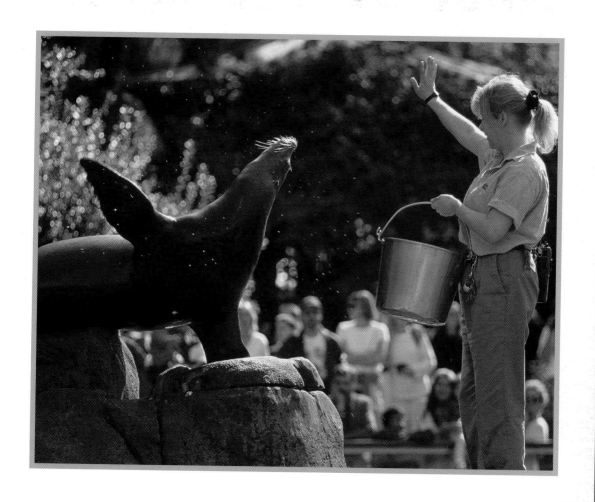

In the zoo, sea lions spend time with **zookeepers**.

People watch zookeepers feed the sea lions.

How Do Sea Lions Sleep?

Sea lions sometimes sleep on land.

Many sea lions sleep together in sunny places.

Sea lions sometimes sleep in the water.

They float with their **snouts** sticking out.

What Sounds Do Sea Lions Make?

Sea lions can roar like lions.

That is how they got their name.

Sea lions can make a honking sound.

They can also bark.

How Are Sea Lions Special?

Sea lions are good swimmers.

But they can also use their **flippers** to walk on land.

Sea lions are good learners.

Zookeepers can teach them to do many things.

Quiz

Do you remember what these sea lion parts are called?

Look for the answers on page 24.

? ? ?

?

Picture Glossary

colony
page 10

mammal
page 4

snout
pages 7, 17

ear flap
page 7

pup
pages 8, 9

squid
pages 12, 13

flipper
pages 6, 20

shore
page 10

zookeeper
pages 13, 15, 21

Note to Parents and Teachers

Reading for information is an important part of a child's literacy development. Learning begins with a question about something. Help children think of themselves as investigators and researchers by encouraging their questions about the world around them. In this book, the animal is identified as a mammal. A mammal is an animal that is covered with hair or fur and that feeds its young with milk from its body. The symbol for mammal in the picture glossary is a dog nursing its babies. Point out that although the photograph for mammal shows a dog, many other animals are mammals—including humans.

Index

Answers to quiz on page 22

snout
whiskers
ear flap
flippers